Entrances

Also by George Messo:

From the Pine Observatory

GEORGE MESSO

Entrances

↘

- New Poems -

Shearsman Books
Exeter

Published in the United Kingdom in 2006 by
Shearsman Books Ltd
58 Velwell Road
Exeter EX4 4LD

www.shearsman.com

ISBN-10   0-907562-90-6

ISBN-13   978-0-907562-90-0

Copyright © George Messo, 2006.

The right of George Messo to be identified as the author of this work has been asserted by him in accordance with the Copyrights, Designs and Patents Act of 1988. All rights reserved. No part of this publication may be reproduced, stored in a retrieval system, transmitted in any form or by any means, electronic, mechanical, photocopying, recording or otherwise, without the prior permission of the publisher.

Acknowledgements

"Winter by the Choruh River" appeared in *United Nations Dialogue Through Poetry 2001 Anthology*, edited by Taylor, Davineni & Srivastava, Rattapallax Press, New York.

"Visiting the Greek House of Yashar Chalik, with Musa Kul" was commissioned by the magazine *Kül* as part of the exhibition *40 photographs, 40 writers* and first shown on the Ankara Underground.

Continued on page 83.

The publisher gratefully acknowledges financial assistance from
Arts Council England.

Contents

◥ *Lost in Leaves*

    Winter by the Choruh River   11
    In Ketel Paulsen's House   12
    Mothlike I   13
    Mothlike II   14
    The Orchard at Night   15
    Hotel Paris, Trabzon   16
    A Trabzon Orchard   17
    Entrances   18
    Shenyuva   19
    Farewell Memur Bey   21

◥ *Midday Stars*

    The Beautiful Apartments   25
    First there is Morning   26
    The Use and Meaning of Tranquility   27
    Teahouse Routine   28
    Going to Rize   29
    Fruit Music   30
    Night Journey   31
    Poem   32

◥ *Frosting Glass*

    The Tree's High Leaves   39
    Georgia in the 11th Century   40
    Declivity   41

Articles of Faith	42
Two Siberias	43
The Tideless Sea	44
Sleepwalking/Medical Notes	48
Fragments of a Black Sea Mountain Poem	49

↘ *Consent to Cloud*

Mesnevi Street	53
Notes from the Haft Awrang	54
We Are Tired And the Mystery Too Big	57
Visiting the Greek House of Yashar Chalik, with Musa Kul	58
Temperaments	60
I Close My Eyes	61
Weather Like This	62

↘ *Air*

quarter	67
breath	68
backstreets & boulevards	69
ochre. auburn. scarf	71
too little where	74
lom	80

Notes   82

in memory of
Yaşar Çalık

↘

for
Musa Kul
Ferhat Öztürk
Mustafa Kılıç
&
Durukan Ordu

Lost in Leaves

Winter by the Choruh River

A woman is rowing across a dark rift.
The scarf she wears is blue. But
she does not see me here among the trees.
The snow is thick as cream and the river
a black cloud she steers across.

On the far bank smoke rises blue from her house.
Blue of her scarf, blue of the wood-smoke rising.

In Ketel Paulsen's House

for Stephen McLoughlin

October on the high plateau. My friends
and I are gazing, half-surprised,
through Ketel Paulsen's window.
                                          It's colder
than we know: ice in the hazel grove
a barrel splits to hold.
                         Yet surprised,
by sudden snow we scarce expect,
                                    and moved,
already,
      to the verge of enterprise.

Mothlike I

For once I know we
have to live and why.

A thought entirely you,
each day makes spaces
shaped for inner things.

Tonight, a Trabzon balcony
in spring. The sky has peeled
a segment set in time.

Mothlike II

Still it is something the storm can wake us;
chords of driven rain strike the window.

We rise and thumb around the darkness,
oblique in unlit skins, and cling to it,

what love there is, close enough
to sense how far we've moved apart.

The Orchard at Night

The walk uphill inspired you.
– Others know the world turns slow going up. –
You closed yourself off from the town,
pursued by fusts and Autumn smells.

Darkness spat figures along the path.
Men with beards and suspicions
– of what they were not yet sure.
But wait. You were just an idea
of a thing they'd truly hate, given time.

Move on. Look back. Ahead,
the sky turned red behind the trees
and the mountain sang once more of home.
Behind, a future of holes you'd return through.

A comet appeared in the sky that night.
You trembled and slept.
Why had you gone there?
Didn't I say you'd be cold?

Hotel Paris, Trabzon

for Mustafa Kılıç

Rumour is I'm leaving.
My room is shaped like a cage
and the sun puts a fist through the window.

But I, who only want to smoke,
know nothing, and light my cigarette.

I don't want to leave.
I want to smoke.

After Apollinaire

A Trabzon Orchard

Earth smells rising up.
A week of rain unbinds
a summer mountain, cools
a sense left sleeping there.

In groves, I knew him once,
coaxing fruit or yielding grass
– some esoteric scheme
to stir the inside out of life.

A man alone is almost mythic.
The city closing in could not
subvert him. And who can touch
him now, among the hazel,

lost in leaves and God?

Entrances

for Michael Lowenthal

All morning climbing down the wooded gorge
who knows sometimes the loneliness you move towards
or where you unexpectedly are lost in mud and greenage
finally to be among the river's thickest coils

in silence oh my God and nothing there but beauty
not enough the silvering of water-quiffs or fish
which rise imperceptibly to flies or what
you think may even be seed-pods floating by.

Bored, as you are, with constant re-description
no longer swayed by frightful sounds –
named inner lives, imagined selves
– you opt to leave the afternoon
and step, one naked foot, into the Choruh river.

Unmistakably it is light
fading or else failing always
into which you will emerge –

the wish to be there, suddenly real,
puts everything in its place.

Shenyuva
with apologies to Li Shang-Yin

I
At night
standing by the river,
the sound of water,

and the water itself
swollen by sudden rain
falling in the summer pool.

II
You ask how long before we catch a fish.
Still we cannot say. But the night rains
swell the summer pool.

III
Day after day we come
and cannot move the shy trout
with our flies and quaint philosophy.

IV
Would you say
the mystery that we are
to ourselves

is any less so here
at night
when the big fish move

unheard
for the sound of the body
they move within . . .

V
And how long now before we too
talk back to the time we stood
beside the falls in Shenyuva.

Farewell Memur Bey

Nights are long and cold.
Say, if they ask,
he followed a heart.

Red nails
and a torn cloud
mark the trail.

Midday Stars

The Beautiful Apartments

> *The thought working its way towards the light.*
> – Ludwig Wittgenstein, 1946

In the empty block
across the lake from here
you notice first a light
go on go off go on again.

You wonder who
at this late hour
stirs in rooms
darkness uninhabits.

And then yourself, alone,
gazing from a room
towards the light
across the lake from here.

First There is Morning

The clouds in you anoint a blue mood.
And you say you woke early with a feeling
of smallness like fear, newly made. And I
in my own cocoon woke late from desert thoughts
and sky-parades, dwarfed by expansion.

So we wake at opposite ends of ourselves
in a city which is always Ankara
and the weather born in you
rises in me like fog black from the mouth
as I go down the seven flights of stairs
through the vein of a cold December apartment.

Today is not the day to leave. By some concocted chance
in a smoke-filled tea-house far from now, we'll understand
who sent us here, and why, and what it meant to stay.

The Use and Meaning of Tranquility

for Bjarni Bjarnason

Who except ourselves could come between us now
turning from the empty road and the car doors
swing out on nothingness, stopped, because you say there are
      sparks
from the hood what could they be like embers
weather-blown or slow moving heat from the plain
each an orange glow. And so we unwind
our own embroidery with sun to hand and rising
from a snaking coast-bound-mountain-road
the sea's humidity the faultless clockwork
of an hour each second motioning our end
our moving close to primacy or where it was
we started fighting from, that you could almost laugh
when the grief finally drains so tired
to have cried so long, seemingly to stumble upon
that dominion of serene oblivion: tranquility, knowing the
      journey
outruns its own allegory and finds for us another use
when everything we have we own, not sparks but flies
in a sheet of light, the sun, these midday stars:
flies in a sheet of light.

Teahouse Routine

Fabrics weaved on entering
quilt their cigarette smoke.
A four-legged wooden stool's
held out, then held back,
placed beside the stove.
A hand laid flat
to its wickered seat
only fingers rising falling
gestures you to sit
and though you've lived
here five long years
the account book's always out.
Is it green they ask where you're from
and then as green as this?
                              Their faces
turn from the circle in which you sit.
But the windows are myopic,
their village talk has vaporized
– you cannot see outside –
and clouds what might be otherwise seen.

Going to Rize

Red. I came here in the spring,
your Black Sea garden tilting north.
Rain was in our minds, and something
else we thought it might be worth

our while to say. Unsaid. Instead
the one sense turned to everything
was smell. Beads of musk, your red
dress, rain-soaked, holding the scent's sting.

Fruit Music

The cherry tree
and its body-buds
quote pleasure.

Quote "body"
and it buds
the cherry pleasure.

The pleasure tree
buds and quotes
"cherry
        cherry
                cherry."

Night Journey

It's you who cannot sleep
on the night bus
moving miles through cubic black.

The bed you'd dream
is warm and small
but unreachable by dawn.

In every roadside house
lights go out
before we've passed.

Poem

I
In early light　　　burning off a dew
Afghan master　　　Hakim Sanai

himself alone,　　　and prone,
is lying　　　　　　on the ground.

II
The unborn forest   stirs
and moves   beneath him.

What purpose   does he think
he lies there   symbol of?

III
Out to catch   the hare
he dreamt   would reappear

at dawn,   if suddenly
he'd lunge   to life –

the buzzard   of his feral soul
take flight,   thrash the living air,

dust clouds   everywhere!
Ascending thermals   raise him

like a flag,   to eye
the shifting wheat   he'll plummet through

and smite   his dreamt-up heart.

IV
Sanai it was   who said
the book of ourselves   is in us
waiting   to be read.

V
Both bird   and hare
and man   and hare
are one.   What
purpose   did I think
I made them   symbol of?

Frosting Glass

The Tree's High Leaves

Unreachable.
Property of birds and sun.
Let none of us have news
from the high leaves . . .

from the Turkish of Melih Cevdet Anday

Georgia in the 11th Century

I
Your name for it is 'pudze'
a plot of land, fields,
a sodden marsh.
Forests owned by all.

Beneath the earthen roof,
your several rooms.
The sting of pig-piss
fizzing in the dark.

II
Arab geographers
wrote of orchards,
of turnips
heaped in cities,

hearsay of a mill
on the Mtkvari river.

Declivity

He spoke a peculiar dialect.
The ruined monastery
was now his farm.
Cowshit filled the nave.

Sound of stone
I thought he said
falling through air,
falling through the centre of a well.

Then
I wasn't sure what he'd said.
Frescoes, devils-full of naked flesh,
women baring breasts.

A well-centred stone
falling through air,
falling through the centre of sound.

Articles of Faith

for Kenny Fountain

Hands
which cannot help
be placed together like a bowl,
or else the lake,
the way it's held there by the land,
and then the land itself.

Say,
then say again.
The lake looks in on darkness.

Say,
and then again,
the lake to which you move a sense was once
the smallest brook or stream or what you will
that ever sluiced away among the desert shrub
and that – a place you do not know – is where
the thing we're stirred to talk about
is formed between its banks, *a* lake.
And so, *the* land, *a* land where it, *the* lake,
is held together like your palms,
suppliant in its bowl of dust
is ruminant, exhausted, without speech,
the thing we'll talk about.

Two Siberias

1. An essay

This essay is the story of two Chekhovs. The she of it after a while deports to a distant place. Let's call it Siberia. One day, today, the he of it is alone, again. The story does not go well. So much did, in her life, happen. Truth was a mystery and therefore useless, the gangrenous toes themselves an unwanted fact. In the end the woman who is, however, a bourgeois eats only holes, becomes whole.

2. A Turk in the Hotel Gulag

In Moscow, morbid, sick for home
You claw the breast of exile.
Siberia is far away,
The night wood mute with snow.

But this is not your shame
To fear death and dream it.
You never lost your faith for long.
You got off the train, Brodsky stepped on.

Siberia is far away,
The night wood mute with snow.

The Tideless Sea

I

At the long journey's end
you unfurled the sea,

slipped between wave and shore,
made this your bed and slept.

And the sea at last was silent.

II

A bird stopped motionless in flight
and an affair that had not yet even begun

somehow came to a tragic end.
You slept and imperceptibly

the world grew old without you.

III

This is how we recall
and how our mourning you

finds its metaphor
when once you were more

than the absence that you are.

IV

Once more the sun
beats a path to our door.

Its ancient wheel rolls across rooftops.
But there is no more this and that,

except an overwhelming hiss so loud
as the sun goes down in the sea.

It rasped your heart and split the moon in two.
We cannot say we are happy now.

Sleepwalking / Medical Notes

Doors snap in the wind.
Three days ill,
and it is snowing.

Ungaretti said it first:
The pointlessness of solitude.
Yashar, whose name means life,

you are three years dead
and I am still in Ankara's State Hospital.

They think I'm lunatic, call me somnambulist,
say I ate the sun and became darkness.

*

Doors snap in the wind, doors
you could leave my room to close,
wake me from the recent past,
as if from a light sleep.

Faces crowd the portal:
snow in their hair, breath frosting the glass.

Fragments of a Black Sea Mountain Poem

His pocketbook. We read of "smallness overlooked", of gathering mass, "no greater than a stone, before an edge it's falling from." And would I look, asks Dr Kul, the matter of another's mind, me being of the mountain going kind? In here, I say, we do not always speak the things we mean to say. He was, for one, thinking "çiğ" when mis-translating "avalanche." In point of fact and from the fragments here dislodged we see him meaning "landslide", "rockfall", "wave of stone".

What hope in all of this? asks Dr Kul. We notice only smallnesses, as if the hill intrudes. But what is this!? "O merciful God, everything is almost too much itself. Here we go again with our small hands. The mountain does not know us, but still we tug at its sleeve."

Consent to Cloud

Mesnevi Street

Pale light and the late evening.
Empty cars, wide open streets.
Shadows rise across the city,
as I go out to join them . . .

Notes from the Haft Awrang

1. The Wise Old Man

Not what they are but what they seem,
Scenes from the far side of a dream.

The wise old man chides a foolish youth.
Staring through the boy the old man finds

The hare behind a rise half its size
Gazing at the rock-toned mountain fox.

The fox looks skyward, finds the bear
Fixing on the deer. The deer in turn

Finds perching doves below a racing cloud.
The formulas are the same, after all

What are birds without a tree in which
To be themselves the mirror of human

Company? There is for once no human-
Headed horse to say what must be said.

While the old man chides a foolish youth
Wisdom, instead, speaks with a bird's mouth.

2. Yusuf Tends His Flocks

The many-birded plane tree's three toned leaves
shade would-be prophet Yusuf's flaming head.

Zulaykha watches from an ornate trellis tent.
The unsaddled mare is dapple-blue and see

what now she seems to say: geometry is beauty!
How precisely this old servant carrying sticks and

knotted clouds is robbed in blue, the goat
observing Yusuf also blue. Zulaykha watches

Yusuf watch his flock. Between them a tree,
and in the tree, a nest. Two eggs. Yusuf

and Zulaykha. In miniatures of this time
birds in flight are birds falling . . .

3. The Flight of the Tortoise

There was once a tortoise who lived in a marsh with two geese. They were all very good friends. One day the geese decide it is time to spread their wings and fly south for winter. The tortoise is overwhelmed with grief at the thought of his friends' departure. The geese fly off to a nearby tree and soon return each holding the end of a torn off branch. They implore the tortoise to bite down on the middle of the stick and away they go, high above the earth. The tortoise is happy. The geese are happy. The three are happy, happy, happy. After a while they approach a large and splendid city. – Is it Isfahan? Well, yes, it could be. – The people of Isfahan gaze in wonderment and surprise at the flying tortoise. The tortoise calls down to them not to envy him in his flight, and letting go his hold, falls, crashing to the ground.

The moral of the story is this: think before you open your mouth, or don't be a tortoise, or whenever you see two geese carrying a tortoise clamped to a stick, don't point, don't stare too long, take wonderment as it comes. Thank Allah for the souls of geese, for the courage of a tortoise.

We are Tired and the Mystery too Big

Come into the garden, he said.
But there was no garden.

Visiting the Greek House of Yashar Chalik, with Musa Kul

I

We come we do
not know for the last time,

a city's edge fenced out,
a pavement's terminal gate.

This is where you made a home
and where the home made you.

The garden is a lapis-work
of leaf and branch and stem.

II

What's overlooked, or left behind
when a house walks out on life?

A kind of grief, its slow increase
and contradictory urge

to speak, and hold its tongue.
We will not say you're dying now,

so neither of us know.
The husked vowels you chase

are your own voice, calling out
"Kübraa! Kübraa!"

Where does she go
this girl of yours

lost among the hazel grove
when there you sleep in grass

and wake to a different word?
Your hair unkempt,

but still it is your hair
and the garden ours for now.

Temperaments

There is a bird. It wants to land but cannot.
Imagine, fatigue overcoming even fear.

A willingness to face the sun and be blind.

I Close My Eyes

There are simpler things returning to us. Close your eyes. Whoever it is we think we are across this landscape making us, a different voice is speaking to you now. You're on the coastal road. The blue of yet another sky is veining through its cloud. Your clothes, electric wet, are charged against your skin. We're toeing the lip of a hole we'll spend a lifetime falling in. I close my eyes, and only then the sound restates the place: heavy tread of bodies down from hill farms loaded up with roots; wet-releasing earth-oils; herb-rich voices; Black Sea gulls. And who are they to think our knowing them makes a difference to the world or way our seeing eye turns in upon itself.

There are simpler things returning now. Close your eyes. Whoever it is we think we are across this space where language makes us foreign to ourselves . . . I close my eyes. You're on the coastal road. I have taken from its found abode your heart and place it here with me.

Weather Like This

Take one last look.
A man is walking out to sea, one standing on the shore.
And those who brought you here have left.

*

You are in the garden of Yavuz Sultan Selim.
Mountains hold the sky up like a child.
Found in the shade of cedar trees,

a sole fig-tree bears its single fruit.
If you lay down under that very tree
perchance you may catch this fig

as it falls through seven centuries,
the Sultan gazing out of his past
as you stare back at him.

But your shoes are soaked and your overcoat smells of dog.
History will not let you in.

There are women moving upward under sticks,
mountains on their backs.

You suppose there will be fires
in the homes of Karlik, hill of snowfullness.

*

If you cannot get it right, this way
of feeling what there is, then nothing.

Wood smoke rising into cloud,
through mist and (lightly spoken) rain.
Yağmur, Sis, Bulut.

Insist on meaning. Consent to cloud.
The language is all over you.
Let mountains hold you like a child

Air

*Air, then, is something alive like a rock only quicker, I thought,
and sat light-headed in the presence of a great surprise.*

Anthony Piccione

quarter

I leave the house
        – don't leave the house! they say
                but the house is left

to stillness knocking on time.
        I take the track
                by shepherd Orhan's house

– don't take the track! they say
but the track takes me.

their words have wings
        and the voice moves out
                like a migratory bird.

I think I hear it fall
        – don't hear at all, they say,
                don't hear . . .

I leave this house
        – don't leave the house! they say.
                but the house is left

to stillness knocking on time.

breath

throw it then.
and where you are is where
the stone's leaving shapes an empty hand.
language, and the air through which
its falling makes an arc, says

thrown, a stone-fall moves the lake.

how far in even time
can ripples go, the outward
moving sense of place, of state or home? –
as if the stones or waves or waters know.

backstreets & boulevards

I must have drifted off.

hours tightened on the night drum.

crickets and the click of heels –

the street knows best whose feet they wear.

you enter a shop selling only loneliness.

the room pulsates to a swarm of flies

swollen around a naked bulb.

just think

you have never been the person you are now

and yet

you have never known yourself better.

you think

if there were no God

you wouldn't need protecting.

nor the boy going down to the beach,

throwing sticks for a dog that follows him.

wave after wave and the stick

so far from sight only gulls to mock & shit

on a barking dog who barks alone

at the end of a derelict beach.

then what if,

if there were no boy,

no dog,

no beach?

only sea

and your strangled breath beneath it,

air

moving up from silence into sound

with no one to hear it.

ochre. auburn. scarf.

ochre.

your need
to know
through tone
the touch
of sand
on skin.

auburn.

is a scarf
curled
shell-like
wind
you cannot feel
has made;
the lesser
of its tone
more wonder-filled
in what it tells
than what
is told of it.

scarf.

through touch
to know,
on skin
you cannot feel:
a scarf,
the lesser
of its telling tone,
the lesser
of its wind-like
wonder-fill,

to know
what need
has made
of what it tells,

to know
an auburn
ochre scarf.

too little where

I

How suddenly it changed. Was barely light when he set out; time, he hardly knew. Trees ahead. An overwhelming wood. The freshness of his walk. A landscape closing in to accent each particular thing.

II

He paused by the torn exclosure fence. And dazzlement came quickly to his sense . . . A breath, long-held. His unremembered spot where upland steppe held out: sun-emblazened pines.

Slow at first, his walk began. Then stride increasing stride. Already faint but sure, a murmur through the wood. Each leaf would cup to hold it, pass it on.

III
Perhaps a voice, mistook.

IV

When he thought, some liquid mass took form. Burned a while beneath his brow. Transfigured it. So far he'd come. So far.

A second held. And wide.

In and out of grief. All night he searched the steppe. A second heard. Or only half-believed he heard. All evening with the burn.

Worlds of sound. Then night's infernal thrum. The one-time music played across his lips. Whispered it. But heard. For sure... A sound, could set his thinking back a century.

V

To the house and Mahtab, waiting. Sleepless. Loose. Unnerving eyes.

"I worried." Words she spoke consumed themselves. "Where this time?"

Where he always went. But lied. "Further out." A wooded cwm he knew and felt again the bruising air. Snow dissolving from his cheeks. Recalled again the birch, embossed in ice.

And the storm. It's sudden gain.

Bound awhile.

VII

From the window glass, scraped ice numbed her fingers. In early light she'd watched him go. Away from her.

Half accusation, half plea, she'd asked, "Where were you all this time?" falling short of all she wished to know or hear him say; how the waiting ground her to a dust. Scattered.

And as he starred at her now, she re-lived how, in the cocoon of her own grief, that particular morning sun had pricked her sense, as he made his way by the field-path – her watching – picked his way through pines, dew-wet, the winter sun rising with him.

And something inexplicable rose in her too, shook the very air it moved within, and from nothing imperceptible charge took form, articulated space. A blistered void, voiced.

He was already too far gone to hear the scream.

lom

sun sets rumour
deep inside the glacier:

it is meltwater May.
the river has its ticket

to the sea.
standing on a bridge

the fish know nothing of us
rising in water still cold

enough to shock-out souls
or jog the pool's thawing

winter memory.
say nothing. rivers

are the earth's
unceasing clocks.

everything is beginning.
everything at an end.

Notes

Shenyuva: mountain village on the banks of the Fırtına (Storm) River, near Çamlihemşin, in the eastern Black Sea mountains. Shenyuva means literally happy (şen) home (yuva).

Farewell Memur Bey: "memur" is a civil or public servant.

Going to Rize: city east of Trabzon, on the Black Sea, pronounced *Reezé*.

Notes from the Haft Awrang: my visual source for these poems was the *Haft Awrang* of Abdul-Rahman Jami, commissioned by the Safavid prince Sultan Ibrahim Mirza and completed 1556-1565. The manuscript is now housed in the Freer Gallery of the Smithsonian Institution, Washington, D.C. Marianna Shreve Simpson's *Haft Awrang: A Princely Manuscript from Sixteenth-Century Iran* (1997) offers the most comprehensive critical history of the manuscript to date.

Weather like This: Yavuz Sultan Selim, known to the West as Selim the Grim, was sometime governor of Trabzon. His former residence is now a library and tea garden.

Yağmur = rain,
Sis = fog/mist,
Bulut = cloud.

Acknowledgements
(continued from copyright page)

Several poems were read in earlier drafts at the Aegean University, Izmir, and subsequently published in *Selves at Home, Selves in Exile: Stories of Emplacement and Displacement* edited by Kırtunç, Silkü, Rose and Erdem (2002). Eight of these poems appeared in the anthology *Framing Reference* (Near East Books, 2001), and six of them in the anthology *Reactions #3* (2002), edited by Esther Morgan, Pen & Inc, England. Some poems have appeared in the anthologies *Listening to the Birth of Crystals* (2003) edited by Corkish & Taylor and *In Our Own Words: A Generation Defining Itself* (2004) edited by Marlow Weaver; others will appear in Andy Brown's forthcoming anthology *The Allotment: New Lyric Poets* (Stride, 2006).

Other poems were first published in *The Journal*, *Kül*, *Le Poète Travaille*, *Magma*, *Metamorphoses*, *Öteki-siz*, *Shearsman*, *Stand*, *Two Rivers Review* and *Yom Sanat*.

Thanks to the Hawthornden Foundation (Scotland), the International Writer's & Translator's Centre of Rhodes (Greece), and The Baltic Centre, Gotland (Sweden), for residency fellowships.

www.ingramcontent.com/pod-product-compliance
Lightning Source LLC
Chambersburg PA
CBHW031928080426
42734CB00007B/600